Malaysian Cakes & Desserts

Rohani Jelani

PERIPLUS

Malaysians are well known for having a sweet tooth. Unlike some people who limit themselves to a modest helping of dessert at the end of a meal, or a slice of cake for tea, Malaysians happily indulge in sweet cakes and desserts throughout the day.

It is not uncommon for cakes such as *serimuka* (glutinous rice topped with a coconut custard) or *kuih talam* (a layered rice flour cake) to appear at the breakfast table alongside *nasi lemak* (coconut rice) or a plate of fried noodles. Similarly, a mid-morning coffee break is not complete if it does not include a sugar coated *kuih keria* (sweet potato doughnut) or a roll of *kuih dadar* (a pandan-flavoured pancake filled with a sweet coconut filling).

And what better way to make a blistering afternoon more bearable than by enjoying a cup of hot sweet tea with a selection of delicate cakes or a rich bean broth simmered with fragrant coconut milk and palm sugar?

In the past, searching for a workable *kuih* (cake) recipe was virtually impossible. The making of traditional cakes was almost exclusively the domain of elderly grandmothers and aunts who subscribed to the '*agak agak*' (approximation) method. If one asked nicely, they might oblige with a vague description of a recipe but trying to decipher it was always a challenge.

Traditional cooks rarely measure anything, they instinctively take a handful of this and a cupful of that and mix it all together without any need to glance at weighing scales or recipes. They rely on visual clues, and the consistency of a cake batter, for example, is often described in various degrees of 'thickness'. One is likely to be instructed to dip one's fingers into a particular mixture and then observe how thickly (or thinly) the batter clings to them.

Such esoteric instructions leave modern cooks, accustomed to weighing ingredients out to the last gram, totally bewildered. Recognising this, we have taken these traditional recipes and tested them rigorously, to the point where we could attach precise weights and measures to them so that you, the home cook, can use them with confidence.

Agar powder (*agar-agar*): The most powerful gel-form of all gums and one which is able to withstand high temperatures; a popular setting agent in Malaysia.

Alkali water: Available from supermakets and bakery supply shops, alkali water adds a springy quality to cakes. Omit if not available.

Coconut milk (*santan*): To obtain fresh coconut milk, see Note on page 14. Powdered coconut milk is readily available in supermarkets and Asian stores.

Flour: Various types of flour are used in Malaysian cakes and desserts, most notably rice flour (*tepung beras*), glutinous rice flour (*tepung beras pulut*) and tapioca flour (*tepung ubi*). All are available from Asian food stores.

Ginkgo nut: The yellow green kernel is protected by a hard smooth yellow shell that must be discarded first. A bitter germ inside the nut must also be removed.

Glutinous rice: Two types of glutinous rice are commonly used in Malaysian cakes and desserts: the white grain (*beras pulut*) and the black grain (*pulut hitam*). Glutinous white rice is readily available from Asian food stores, while glutinous black grain rice is sold at speciality stores.

Mung bean (*kacang hijau*): These dried small green beans must be soaked and boiled before use. Sprouted mung beans are the most common source of bean sprouts. Available from large supermarkets and Asian food stores.

Palm sugar (*gula Melaka*): Made from either the aren or coconut palm, this raw sugar has a slightly smoky flavour. Substitute with soft brown sugar.

Pandan leaf (*daun pandan*): Also known as screwpine leaf, pandan (or pandanus) leaves are used to add fragrance to savoury dishes, and green colour to sweet dishes. May be substituted with vanilla essence but the flavour will be different.

Pearl sago: Sago grains impart the characteristic 'frogspawn' texture to many puddings and desserts and are strained and rinsed to rid them of excess starch.

Sweet potato (*keledek*): An orange-coloured tuber which is actually related to *kangkong* (water convulvulus) and not to the potato.

Tapioca tuber (*ubi kayu*): Also known as cassava and manioc, tapioca tubers are most commonly used to obtain starch or flour.

Yam (*ubi keladi*): Also known as taro. This oval, starchy tuber with dark brown skin, and flesh ranging from creamy white to purple, must be peeled and cooked thoroughly as undercooked taro can cause irritations in the throat and mouth.

Inti (Coconut Filling)

100 g (2/3 cup) palm sugar, roughly chopped
75 ml (1/4 cup + 1 tablespoon) water
1 pandan leaf, knotted
100 g (1 cup) grated coconut

Makes 1 cup
Preparation time: **20 mins**
Cooking time: **10 mins**

1 Place palm sugar and water in a pan and cook until sugar dissolves. Simmer for 10 minutes until liquid starts to thicken and become syrupy.
2 Add the pandan leaf and grated coconut and continue cooking over low heat for 10 to 15 minutes until the coconut filling is thick and glossy. Most of the liquid should have evaporated. Cool and use as desired. Keeps well if stored in a covered container in the fridge.

Palm Sugar Syrup

100 g (2/3 cup) palm sugar, roughly chopped
75 ml (1/4 cup + 1 tablespoon) water
1 pandan leaf, tied into a knot

Makes 1/2 cup
Preparation time: **20 mins**
Cooking time: **10 mins**

1 Place palm sugar and water in a pan, together with the pandan leaf. Bring liquid to a boil, then reduce heat to a simmer.
2 Simmer over low heat for 10 minutes or until liquid thickens slightly and is 'syrupy'.

Pandan Juice

6–8 large pandan leaves
150 ml (2/3 cup) water

Makes 1/2 cup
Preparation time: **20 mins**
Cooking time: **10 mins**

1 Rinse pandan leaves and, using kitchen scissors or a sharp knife, cut leaves into 2-cm (3/4-in) lengths.
2 Place leaves and water in the jug of an electric blender or chopper and process until pulverized. Pour through a fine strainer and discard solids. Measure out the required amount of juice as specified in the recipe.

For maximum flavour and colour, choose mature, dark green leaves over younger, light green ones.

How to make a pandan brush

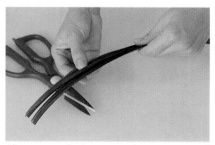

Align two pandan leaves together, one on top of the other.

Fold the leaves over each other, about 12 cm (5 in) long.

Tie one end tightly with a rubber band or length of string to make a handle.

Using scissors, cut open the looped end of the leaves.

Use the scissors to snip the loose ends to make a brush.

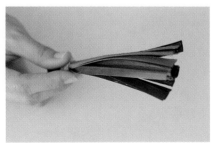

Use the pandan brush for greasing pans or cake moulds.

Sweet Potato Pudding
(Bubur Ca Ca)

1 small yam (taro), about 200 g (6 1/2 oz)
1 small sweet potato, about 200 g (6 1/2 oz)
1 pandan leaf, tied into a knot
750 ml (3 cups) water
250 ml (1 cup) coconut milk
100 g (3 1/2 oz) white sugar or chopped palm sugar
Pinch of salt
2 ripe bananas, peeled and cut diagonally into 1-cm
   (1/2-in) slices

1 Peel the yam and sweet potato and cut into 1-cm
(1/2-in) cubes. Rinse well.
2 Place yam and sweet potato in a medium-sized
saucepan with the pandan leaf and water and
bring to the boil. Reduce heat to medium and cook
until the yam and sweet potato are tender, about
15 to 20 minutes.
3 Add coconut milk, sugar and salt and return to the
boil. Add the sliced bananas and cook for a further
5 minutes. Serve warm or cold.

*Pearl sago may be added to the bubur ca ca to give it
an interesting texture. Rinse 1 tablespoon sago in a
sieve and add at the end of step 2. Then cook the
mixture for 5 minutes before adding the coconut milk.*

Serves 5 to 8
Preparation time: **20 mins**
Cooking time: **30 mins**

Black Rice Pudding (Bubur Pulut Hitam)

150 g (2/3 cup) black glutinous rice (*pulut hitam*)
1 litre (4 cups) water
1 pandan leaf, tied into a knot
120–140 g (1/2 cup or more) white sugar (depending on sweetness preferred)
250 ml (1 cup) coconut milk
1/4 teaspoon salt

1 Pick the rice over for husks and any foreign particles. Wash in several changes of water and then cover with fresh water. Leave to soak for 30 minutes.
2 Drain rice and add 1 litre (4 cups) fresh water. Bring to the boil together with the pandan leaf; then reduce heat to low and simmer until grains are soft and most of the liquid has evaporated, about 1 hour. (The final consistency should be creamy and porridge-like; if it looks dry, stir in a cup of water.)
3 Add sugar and cook for another 10 minutes before removing pan from heat.
4 Combine the coconut milk and salt in a small pan. Heat gently, stirring constantly, until it reaches boiling point. Remove pan from heat. Serve the porridge in small bowls with a spoonful of coconut milk swirled over the top.

Serves 4 to 6
Preparation time: **40 mins**
Cooking time: **1 hour 10 mins**

Red Bean Broth with Dried Tangerine Peel

150 g (3/4 cup) dried red beans (azuki beans)
1 1/2 litres (6 cups) water
5-cm (2-in) piece dried tangerine peel
100–140 g (1/2 cup or more) white sugar (depending on sweetness preferred)

1 Pick beans over for any foreign particles and wash well in several changes of water. Cover with water and leave to soak for 30 minutes.
2 Drain beans and replace with 1 1/2 litres (6 cups) fresh water. Bring to the boil, reduce heat to medium and cook until beans are soft, about 1 hour. Add the tangerine peel half-way through the cooking. Sweeten to taste.

Serves 4 to 6
Preparation time: **35 mins**
Cooking time: **1–1 1/2 hours**

Sweet Potato in Ginger Syrup

350 g (11 1/2 oz) orange and/or yellow sweet potatoes
1 litre (4 cups) water
1 cm (1/2 in) ginger, thinly sliced
1 pandan leaf, tied into a knot
80–120 g (1/3–1/2 cup) caster sugar (depending on sweetness preferred)

1 Peel sweet potatoes and cut into slices 1 cm (1/2 in) thick. Cut these into strips 1 cm (1/2 in) wide and then slice diagonally to form diamond shapes. (Alternatively, cut sweet potatoes into 1-cm (1/2-in) cubes.)
2 Rinse sweet potato pieces, then place in a medium-sized pan with the water, ginger and pandan leaf. Bring to the boil, then reduce heat to medium and cook until sweet potato pieces are tender. Remove ginger and pandan leaf.
3 Sweeten to taste and serve warm or cold.

Serves 4 to 6
Preparation time: **15 mins**
Cooking time: **20 mins**

Barley, Ginkgo Nut & Bean Curd Broth

50 g (1/4 cup) pearl barley
1 1/2 litres (6 cups) water
200 g (1 1/2 cups) ginkgo nuts (with shells)
1 pandan leaf, tied into a knot
2 sticks dried beancurd (*fu chook*) sheets
100–140 g (1/2 cup or more) white rock, or granulated white, sugar

1 Rinse barley in several changes of water until water runs clear. Place in a roomy pan with the water and leave to soak for 20 minutes.

2 Meanwhile, carefully crack the ginkgo nut shells and remove nuts. Place in a small pan, cover with water and bring to the boil. Remove pan from heat, drain water and run cold water over the nuts—this makes it easier to peel off the papery skins covering the nuts. There is also a germ within the ginkgo nuts which needs to be removed as it is bitter. You can do this by either splitting the nut into half and removing it, or by gently pushing it out using a toothpick.

3 Place the prepared ginkgo nuts into the pan of soaked barley and bring to the boil. Simmer until tender, about 45 minutes, adding the pandan leaf half-way through the cooking.

4 When barley and ginkgo nuts are tender, crumble the beancurd skin into the broth and cook for another 10 to 15 minutes. Sweeten to taste. Serve either warm or cold.

If using tinned ginkgo nuts, add to the broth when the barley has softened.

Serves 4 to 6
Preparation time: **20 mins**
Soaking time: **20 mins**
Cooking time: **1 hour 15 mins**

Pandan Layered Cake (Kuih Talam)

Green layer

50 g (1/3 cup + 2 table-
spoons) rice flour

4 teaspoons tapioca flour

1 tablespoon green pea
flour

160 g (2/3 cup + 4 tea-
spoons) white sugar

100 ml (1/3 cup) pandan
juice (see page 4)

250 ml (1 cup) water

1/4 teaspoon alkali water

Coconut cream layer

2 tablespoons rice flour

1 tablespoon + 2 tea-
spoons green pea flour

1/4 teaspoon salt

250 ml (1 cup) coconut
milk

1 To make the green layer, combine the rice, tapioca and green pea flours in a bowl and mix in the sugar. Add the pandan juice and water and mix until well combined and smooth. Add alkali water. Strain mixture into a double boiler or bowl sitting on top of simmering pan of water. Stir until mixture starts to thicken and remove bowl from heat. Pour into a 16-cm (6 1/2-in) square cake tin. Steam until set, about 20 minutes (when you tilt the tin, the mixture shouldn't wobble). Set aside.

2 To make the coconut cream layer, combine the rice and green pea flours, and salt. Gradually pour in the coconut milk, stirring well until smooth. Strain into a double boiler and stir the mixture over low heat. Remove from heat as soon as it begins to thicken.

3 Remove the tin containing the green layer from the steamer and blot off excess moisture from the top by gently pressing a sheet of kitchen paper over it, then pour the coconut layer over. Steam for another 15 minutes. Cool thoroughly before cutting.

To obtain fresh thick coconut milk, add 125 ml (1/2 cup) water to the grated flesh of one coconut and squeeze. To obtain fresh thin coconut milk, squeeze the grated flesh with another 625 ml (2 1/2 cups) water.

Makes one 16-cm (6 1/2-in) square cake
Preparation time: **20 mins**
Cooking time: **1 hour**

Steamed Caramel Cake

150 g (2/3 cup) fine granulated sugar
100 ml (1/2 cup less 5 teaspoons) hot water
70 g (2 1/4 oz) butter or margarine, melted
75 ml (1/3 cup + 2 teaspoons) evaporated milk
1 egg, beaten
150 g (1 1/4 cups) plain flour
1 level teaspoon bicarbonate of soda
Pinch of salt
70 g (1/4 cup + 2 teaspoons) fine granulated sugar

Makes one 16-cm (6 1/2-in) cake
Preparation time: 30 mins
Cooking time: 30–40 mins

1 Place the 150 g (2/3 cup) of sugar in a small heavy-based saucepan and heat gently until sugar melts and caramelizes to a nutty, golden brown colour. Take care to keep pan on very low heat to avoid burning the caramel and remove pan from heat once it reaches a golden brown colour.

2 Pour the hot water onto the caramel. (Be careful not to get burned from the sputtering caramel—a good precaution is to wrap the hand holding the jug or cup of water in a cloth.) Boil caramel for a few minutes until completely melted and a syrup is obtained. Allow syrup to cool and pour it out into a measuring cup—you need 160 to 170 ml. If you have less, indicating that you may have boiled and evaporated off more liquid than necessary, add a little water to make up the specified quantity.

3 Add the melted butter, milk and beaten egg to the cooled caramel syrup and stir well to combine.

4 Sift the flour, bicarbonate of soda and salt into a mixing bowl. Stir in the sugar. Make a well in the centre and pour in the liquid. Gradually incorporate the dry ingredients into the liquid, stirring gently with a wooden spoon or balloon whisk for a smooth batter.

5 Line the base of a 16-cm (6 1/2-in) round or square cake tin with greaseproof paper and brush the base and sides lightly with softened butter. Pour batter into the prepared tin and place in a preheated steamer for 30 minutes or until cake is well risen and a skewer inserted in the middle comes out clean. Do not open the steamer before the 30 minutes is up or risk your cake collapsing.

An alternative way to cook this cake is to bake it in an oven preheated to 170°C (340°F) for 25 to 35 minutes. The result is a slightly darker cake with a delicious crust. An alternative way to present it is to fill small, lightly-buttered tartlet tins or rice wine cups three-quarters full of batter and steam for 15 to 20 minutes (depending on the size of the containers). The yield will also depend on the size and depth of the containers.

Baked Tapioca Cake (Bengka Ubi)

1 kg (2 lb) tapioca tubers
220 g (1 cup) white sugar
400 ml (1 2/3 cups)
   coconut milk
1 egg, beaten (optional)
Pinch of salt

Makes one 16-cm (6 1/2-in)
   cake
Preparation time: 30 mins
Baking time: 40 mins

1 To prepare grated tapioca and tapioca starch, first rinse the tubers under running water to remove any sand and grit. Cut roughly into 6-cm (2 1/2-in) lengths. Skin the tapioca by making a shallow cut from the top to bottom of each piece and then running your finger along the cut to 'lift' off the peel. It should come off in one piece quite easily.

2 Finely grate the tapioca but avoid taking the tough fibre that runs down the centre of the tuber. Weigh the grated tapioca—you should obtain a final yield of 800 g (1 3/4 lb).

3 To rid the tapioca of any bitter juices, squeeze it in a muslin cloth or press in a sieve, collecting the juice in a small bowl (and retaining the grated tapioca). Leave the juice undisturbed for 10 to 15 minutes and then carefully pour off, discarding the liquid on top, leaving behind the tapioca starch the bottom of the bowl.

4 Combine the grated tapioca, tapioca starch, sugar, coconut milk, beaten egg (if using; if not, compensate with an extra 50 ml water) and salt.

5 Lightly brush the insides of a shallow round or square cake tin roughly 16 cm (6 1/2 in) across, with light vegetable oil or butter. Pour the tapioca cake mixture into the tin. Level the top with a spoon and bake in a preheated 200°C (400°F) oven for about 40 minutes or until golden brown.

6 Cool before cutting into 3-cm (1-in) squares.

Skin tapioca by making a shallow cut, run a finger along the cut to 'lift' off the peel.

Finely grate tapioca; avoid the tough fibre that runs down the centre of the tuber.

Press grated tapioca in a sieve, collecting the juice into a small bowl.

Pour off and discard the liquid on top, leaving behind the tapioca starch.

Steam the tapioca and sugar mixture over rapidly boiling water for 20 minutes.

Strain coconut milk sauce to rid it of lumps.

Tapioca Layered Cake (Kuih Talam Ubi)

Bottom layer
200 g (1 1/3 cups) palm sugar, roughly chopped
200 ml (3/4 cup + 1 tablespoon) water
800 g (1 3/4 lb) tapioca tubers

Top layer
400 ml (1 2/3 cups) coconut milk
3/4 teaspoon salt
80 g (1/2 cup + 2 tablespoons) plain flour
1 tablespoon rice flour

Makes one 18-cm (7-in) cake
Preparation time: **40 mins**
Cooking time: **40 mins**

1 To make the bottom layer, place the palm sugar in a saucepan with the water. Cook over gentle heat until sugar dissolves. Strain and leave to cool.

2 Prepare the grated tapioca and tapioca starch according to Steps 1, 2 and 3 on page 18. You should obtain a final yield of 600 g (1 1/3 lb) grated tapioca and a little tapioca starch.

3 In a mixing bowl, combine the grated tapioca, tapioca starch and cooled sugar syrup. Transfer this mixture into a shallow cake tin approximately 18 cm (7 in) across and steam over rapidly boiling water for 20 minutes.

4 Meanwhile, make the coconut layer by combining the coconut milk, salt, plain flour and rice flour, stirring well until free from lumps. Strain through a fine sieve.

5 When the tapioca layer is cooked, carefully blot off any excess moisture from the surface by pressing a paper napkin on it. Pour the coconut layer over the tapioca layer and steam the cake again for another 20 minutes until the top is set. Remove tapioca cake from the steamer and cool thoroughly before cutting into 3-cm (1-in) squares or diamond shapes.

Remove excess moisture from the surface by blotting with a paper napkin.

Pour coconut layer over tapioca layer and steam for another 20 minutes.

Stuffed Rice Flour Cakes (Kuih Koci)

1 quantity coconut filling
(*inti*), (see page 4)
200 g (1 3/4 cups)
glutinous rice flour
200 ml (3/4 cup +
1 tablespoon) thin
coconut milk
1–2 banana leaves
1 teaspoon oil

1 Make the *inti* or coconut filling according to the instructions on page 4 and set aside to cool.
2 Combine the glutinous rice flour and coconut milk in a medium bowl, mixing with the fingers and kneading lightly to form a smooth, pliable dough. Cover with a damp towel to prevent it drying out.
3 Meanwhile, blanch banana leaves for 10 to 20 seconds to soften them and then, using a pair of scissors, cut into rectangles approximately 14 x 21 cm (5 1/2 x 8 in). You will need about 12 pieces. Using a pastry brush or your fingers, lightly oil the inside of the banana leaf rectangles.
4 Pinch off small balls of dough the size of large limes (about 30 g or 1 oz each). Roll by hand into smooth balls and then, pressing with your thumb and forefinger, make a well in the centre of the dough and fill with 1 teaspoon of coconut filling (*inti*). Carefully pinch the dough over to enclose the filling.
5 Fashion the banana leaf into a cone with the oiled side on the inside. Place the filled dough ball in it, pushing it gently to fill the tip of the cone as much as possible. Fold the base neatly.
6 As you finish wrapping the cakes in banana leaves, arrange them on a steamer tray. Steam for 12 to 15 minutes.

Makes 12 cakes
Preparation time: 40–60 mins
Cooking time: 30 mins

Spoon 1 teaspoon of coconut filling (inti) into the well in the dough.

Carefully pinch the dough over to enclose the filling.

Shape the leaf into a cone. Place stuffed dough ball into the cone, pushing it in gently.

Fold the base neatly and place the packet on a steamer tray.

Stuffed Glutinous Rice Balls
(Onde-Onde)

200 g (1 3/4 cups) + 1–2 tablespoons glutinous rice flour
150 ml (2/3 cup) pandan juice (see page 4)
2 tablespoons water
200 g (1 1/3 cups) palm sugar, finely chopped
1/2 teaspoon fine salt
75 g (3/4 cup) grated young coconut

Makes about 20 balls
Preparation time: 30 mins
Cooking time: 20 mins

1 Combine the 200 g (1 3/4 cups) glutinous rice flour, pandan juice and water in a medium-sized bowl, kneading well to form a smooth, pliable dough. Cover dough with a damp towel to prevent it drying out.
2 Bring a pan of water to the boil, then lower heat so that the water simmers gently. Pinch out a ball of dough about 2 cm (3/4 in) across, flatten it into a disc and drop it into the simmering water. When the disc is cooked and rises to the surface, lift it out with a slotted spoon, shake off any excess water and knead the cooked dough evenly back into the main ball of dough. If dough still seems sticky, knead in 1–2 tablespoons of glutinous rice flour.
3 Mix salt and grated coconut together and place on a plate.
4 Pinch off small balls of dough the size of calamansi limes (about 20 g each) and roll in your palms to form smooth balls. Carefully make a small well in the centre of the dough and fill with chopped palm sugar. Pinch dough together to enclose, roll them gently to smoothen and, as you make them, drop them into the simmering water.
5 When the dough balls float to the top, carefully remove them with a slotted spoon and allow any excess water to drip off. Drop the balls into the grated coconut and roll them around to coat evenly. Transfer to a serving plate.

Rice Cakes & Sweet Syrup
(Kuih Lopes)

300 g (1 1/2 cups) raw
glutinous rice
150 ml (2/3 cup)
pandan juice (see
page 4)
1/8 teaspoon lime paste
(wetted lime available
from betel nut
vendors)
100 g (1 cup) grated
coconut
1/4 teaspoon salt
Palm sugar syrup (see
page 4)

1 Wash rice in several changes of water until water
runs clear. Cover with fresh water and soak overnight.
2 Combine pandan juice and lime, ensuring that lime
is completely dissolved. Place rice in a shallow cake
tin and pour in the pandan/lime mixture. Steam for
30 minutes until rice is cooked, flaking the rice up
with a fork, halfway through the cooking time.
3 Meanwhile, make the palm sugar syrup according
to the instructions on page 4. Cool, pour into a small
serving jug and set aside.
4 Divide the rice into two roughly equal portions.
Form each one into a thick sausage shape, wrapping
each roll in a sheet of heavy plastic or aluminium foil.
The idea is to compress the rice as much as possible
so that the roll can be neatly sliced. Tie both ends with
string. You should end up with 2 rolls approximately
14 cm (6 in) long and 4 cm (1 1/2 in) in diameter.
5 Set rolls aside for one hour before cutting into neat
slices 1 cm (1/2 in) thick.
6 Stir the salt into the grated coconut and roll the rice
slices in it until well covered. Serve the rice slices with
the palm sugar syrup.

*This is a simplified method for making Kuih Lopes. The
traditional way entails wrapping the rice up in small
individual parcels and boiling them in water for several
hours.*

Serves 6 to 8
Preparation time: **20 mins + overnight soaking**
Cooking time: **45 mins**

Sweet Potato Doughnuts (Kuih Keria)

350 g (11 1/2 oz) yellow
   or orange-fleshed
   sweet potatoes
75 g (1/2 cup) plain
   flour
1/2 teaspoon baking
   powder
Oil for frying
Caster sugar for rolling

Makes about 12 doughnuts
Preparation time: 40 mins
Cooking time: 40 mins

*It is imperative that the
temperature of the
oil is kept low (the
doughnuts should sizzle
slightly upon contact
with the oil). Frying
doughnuts at too high a
temperature will result
in an unattractive,
blistered appearance.*

1 Scrub sweet potatoes clean under running water.
Place in a pan and cover with a generous amount of
water. Boil until tender—test by inserting a skewer
into the thickest part of the potato: it should go in
without much resistance. Remove sweet potatoes
from water and leave to cool.
2 When cool enough to handle, peel the skins. Mash
sweet potatoes until free from lumps. Pick out any
tough fibres and discard.
3 Sift flour and baking powder together and add to
mashed sweet potatoes, kneading lightly until smooth.
4 Break off small pieces of dough about the size of a
lime (about 30 g or 1 oz each) and roll into smooth
balls, flouring your hands lightly to prevent the dough
from sticking. Flatten the balls slightly and make a hole
through the centre of each one with the floured handle
of a wooden spoon. With your fingers, lightly pat the
edges around the hole for a nice, smooth 'doughnut'
finish. Repeat until dough is used up. Lay the doughnuts
on a lightly-floured tray or cloth as you shape them.
5 Heat oil in a pan or wok over medium heat. The oil
should be about 2 cm (1 in) deep. Keeping the heat on
low, fry the doughnuts until golden brown on both
sides, about 6 to 7 minutes. Drain on absorbent paper.
6 Traditionally, these doughnuts are rolled in cooked,
melted sugar until the sugar crystalizes around them.
An easier, healthier way would be to simply roll them
in caster sugar. Serve soon after making.

Peel and mash sweet potatoes until free from lumps.

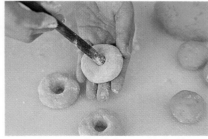

Pierce the centre of each flattened ball with floured handle of a wooden spoon.

Palm Sugar Rice Cakes (Kuih Kosui)

100 g (2/3 cup) palm sugar, roughly chopped
100 ml (1/2 cup less 5 teaspoons) water
60 g (1/4 cup) white sugar
5 tablespoons rice flour
2 tablespoons tapioca flour
1/2 teaspoon alkali water
50 g (1/2 cup) grated young coconut
1/4 teaspoon salt

Serves 4 to 6
Preparation time: 20 mins
Cooking time: 30–50 mins (depending on size)

1 Place palm sugar and water in a small pan over medium heat. Simmer until sugar dissolves then add the white sugar. Stir until dissolved. Strain into a measuring jug/cups and add enough room temperature water to yield a final quantity of 500 ml (2 cups) liquid.

2 Combine the rice flour and tapioca flour together and pour in the cooled sugar syrup and alkali water to form a batter. Strain.

3 Gently heat mixture in a double boiler until it just begins to thicken—don't allow mixture to actually reach the point when it thickens to the texture of custard. Immediately remove pan from the heat.

4 Either pour batter into a shallow 16-cm (6 1/2-in) tray or pour from a jug into small Chinese wine cups, filling them three-quarters full. Steam 40 minutes for the large cake or 12 to 15 minutes, over low to medium heat, for the little cups.

5 Season the grated coconut with salt. Set aside.

6 Allow cakes to cool completely (chill for several hours or even overnight to ease cutting). The large cake can be cut into diamond shapes or squares and then rolled in the grated coconut. The little cakes should be carefully eased out of their cups (carefully run a thin palette-knife around the edges first), placed on a serving plate and each topped with a spoonful of the grated coconut.

Pour batter into shallow tray or small cups.

Rice and Custard Layers
(Serimuka)

Rice layer

300 g (1 1/2 cups) gluti-
nous rice, washed and
soaked overnight
200 ml (3/4 cup +
1 tablespoon) thin
coconut milk
1 teaspoon salt
1 pandan leaf, tied into
a knot

Custard layer

3 medium eggs
200 ml (3/4 cup) coconut
milk
180 g (3/4 cup) white
sugar
100 ml (1/2 cup less
5 teaspoons) pandan
juice (see page 4)
4 teaspoons cornflour
2 tablespoons + 1
teaspoon plain flour

1 To make the rice layer, wash rice in several changes of water until water runs clear. Cover with fresh water and soak for at least 3 hours (or overnight). Rinse and drain rice.

2 Place in a shallow, round or square cake tin, 20 cm (8 in) across. Mix the coconut milk and salt together and add this to the rice. Bury the pandan leaf in the rice and steam over rapidly boiling water until rice is cooked, 20 to 30 minutes (the grains will no longer have any opaque bits).

3 Remove pandan leaves and fluff rice up with a fork. Then, using a folded square of banana leaf or aluminium foil, press the rice down to form an even, compact layer. Steam for another 15 minutes.

4 To make the custard layer, in a mixing bowl, combine the eggs, coconut milk and sugar, stirring with a balloon whisk or wooden spoon. Add the pandan juice, cornflour and plain flour. Stir well until smooth and free from lumps.

5 Strain mixture into a metal bowl and sit this bowl over a pan of gently simmering water. Stir continuously until custard just begins to thicken—do not overcook! Pour this over the rice layer. Steam over very gentle heat (otherwise the custard will have a bubbled surface) until set, about 25 minutes. Avoid opening the steamer as this will only allow heat to escape and lengthen the cooking time.

6 Allow cake to cool completely before cutting.

Makes one 20-cm (8-in) square tray
Preparation time: 20 mins + overnight soaking
Cooking time: 1 1/2 hours

Stir continuously until custard just begins to thicken—do not overcook!

Pour the green custard layer over the rice layer and steam.

Glutinous Rice Cakes with Coconut Jam
(Pulut Tekan)

Pulut Tekan are indigo and white marbled rice cakes served with coconut jam (*kaya*). Extract the indigo colouring from flowers, if desired (see method below), or use blue and red food colouring. Prepare the rice cakes (see recipe page 36) and serve together with coconut jam (*kaya*, recipe below).

How to make coconut jam (*kaya*):

3 medium eggs (to yield 150–170 ml when cracked open)
150 ml (1/2 cup + 5 teaspoons) thick coconut milk
150 g (2/3 cup) granulated sugar
3 pandan leaves, knotted together

1 With a fork or whisk, lightly beat the eggs and coconut milk together. Strain into a double boiler or a metal bowl set over a pan of simmering water. Stir in the sugar and pandan leaves.
2 Cook the kaya over gentle heat, for 1 to 1 1/2 hours, stirring occasionally. (You don't have to stand over it—just give a stir every now and then.) The *kaya* is done when it looks glossy and has thickened to a spreading consistency. Serve in a separate bowl alongside the *pulut tekan*.

How to extract natural indigo colouring:

Traditionally, *pulut tekan* is given its characteristic indigo marbling from a deep indigo coloured juice extracted from *bunga telang* (butterfly, or kordofan, pea flower; L. *clitoria ternatae*). If this is not available, substitute with a few drops of blue colouring mixed with red colouring to produce purple.

1 Prepare 1 to 1 1/2 cups loosely packed *bunga telang* flowers. Rinse flowers to get rid of any insects or sand. Shake off any excess water and then blot dry with paper towels. Gently pluck the purple petals from the green sepals they are attached to.
2 Pound the flowers finely in a mortar and pestle. Without adding any water, squeeze hard with your fingers to extract the purple coloured juice—you may get a mere tablespoon's worth of juice. Set aside.

How to make glutinous rice cakes for Pulut Tekan:

400 g (2 cups) glutinous rice, cleaned, soaked overnight and drained
1 teaspoon salt
150 ml (2/3 cup) thin coconut milk
150 ml (2/3 cup) thick coconut milk
1–1 1/2 cups loosely-packed *bunga telang* (see page 34)
  or 2 drops blue + 1 drop red food colouring
2 pandan leaves, knotted together

Makes one 16-cm (6 1/2-in) square cake
Preparation time: **10 mins + overnight soaking**
Cooking time: **2 hours**

Drain the soaked glutinous rice and place in a shallow heatproof container such as a cake tin or heatproof glass dish. Stir half of the salt into the thin coconut milk until dissolved. Pour into the glutinous rice, bury the knotted pandan leaf in the rice and place container in a pre-heated steamer. Cook undisturbed for 20 minutes.

Meanwhile, stir the remaining salt into the thick coconut milk. Divide this milk into two roughly equal portions and mix one portion with the flower extract (or a few drops of blue and red colouring) to colour it.

Flake the steamed rice with a fork and divide it into two roughly equal portions. Place one portion of the hot rice in a mixing bowl and add the plain coconut milk. Mix well to incorporate.

To the second portion of rice, pour in the coloured coconut milk and mix likewise.

Return the two batches of rice to the steaming container—just place them side by side and continue cooking, undisturbed for another 20 to 30 minutes. By then, the rice should be thoroughly cooked.

Rinse the inside of a 16-cm (6 1/2-in) square cake tin with water and tap off excess. Transfer the cooked rice into the prepared tin, alternating between the white and blue batches to achieve a marbled effect.

When all the rice has been used up, press the rice down to compact it evenly (use a thick fold of banana leaf or aluminium foil for this purpose).

Cover the cake with banana leaves or foil. Then cover with something flat and top with a heavy object such as a granite mortar and pestle, or book, to make the rice compact. Set aside for a couple of hours to allow the rice to become firm. Turn the rice cake out onto a cutting board and cut into neat slices. Serve with coconut milk jam (*kaya*, see recipe on page 34).

Mung Bean Fritters (Kuih Kacang)

200 g (1 cup) dried
  mung beans
750 ml (3 cups) water
1 pandan leaf, tied into
  a knot
120 g (1/2 cup) white
  sugar
50 g (1/2 cup) grated
  coconut
25 g (2 tablespoons +
  2 teaspoons) plain
  flour
Pinch of salt

Batter
6 tablespoons rice flour
2 tablespoons plain
  flour
1/4 teaspoon salt
1 teaspoon sugar
1/8 teaspoon lime
100 ml (1/2 cup less
  5 teaspoons) water

1 Pick beans over for small pebbles or other foreign particles. Wash in several changes of water and then soak for 30 minutes. Drain water and pour in 750 ml (3 cups) fresh water. Add the pandan leaf and bring to the boil. Lower heat and cook beans until soft and most of the water has evaporated, about 45 minutes. Remove the pandan leaf.

2 Add the sugar and stir until dissolved. Cook for 5 minutes until mixture is thick and quite dry. Sprinkle in the flour and salt and stir well to prevent lumps forming. Stir in the grated coconut and cook for another 5 minutes. Remove pan from heat and transfer bean filling onto a shallow tray. Allow mixture to cool.

3 Take heaped tablespoonfuls of the bean mixture and, with lightly-floured hands, roll into small balls before flattening them out slightly into patties about 5 cm (2 in) across. You should get 18 to 20 patties. Cover and refrigerate for 15 to 20 minutes to allow them to firm up.

4 Mix all the batter ingredients together, stirring with a spoon until smooth and free from lumps.

5 Heat oil over medium heat to a depth of 2 cm (1 in). When hot, dip each mung bean patty into the batter and carefully slip into the hot oil, frying for 2 to 3 minutes on each side until the batter is a crisp golden brown. Drain well on absorbent paper and serve warm.

Makes 18–20 patties
Preparation time: **1 hour**
Cooking time: **1 hour 20 mins**

Glutinous Rice Packets with Sweet Coconut Topping (Pulut Inti)

300 g (1 1/2 cups)
   glutinous rice
1/2 teaspoon salt
150 ml (1/2 cup + 5
   teaspoons) coconut
   milk
1 pandan leaf, tied into
   a knot
1 quantitiy coconut filling
   (*inti*, see page 4)
Banana leaves for
   wrapping

Makes 12 parcels
Preparation time: **10 mins
   + overnight soaking**
Cooking time: **50 mins**

1 Pick rice over for husks or foreign particles. Wash in several changes of water until water runs clear. Cover with fresh water and soak overnight.

2 The following day, rinse rice, strain and turn it out onto a shallow cake tin or heatproof dish. Stir salt and coconut milk together and pour over the rice. Bury the pandan leaf in the rice. Steam over rapidly boiling water for 30 minutes, fluffing the rice up with a fork halfway through. Remove rice from steamer.

3 While rice cools, make the coconut filling (*inti*, see page 4).

4 Soften banana leaves by dipping them very briefly in hot water. Wipe well and then cut 12 small squares 4 x 4 cm (1 1/2 x 1 1/2 in) and 12 rectangles 10 x 14 cm (4 x 5 1/2 in).

5 Place a tablespoon of cooked rice in the centre of each rectangle, mounding it slightly in the middle. Place a generous teaspoon of coconut filling on each little square of banana leaf and place this on the rice. Fold the leaf on either side and tuck both ends under, to enclose the rice. You should just be able to see a little bit of coconut filling from the top of the parcel.

Cut banana leaves into small squares and rectangles.

*Place rice on a rectangle, top with a small square leaf then with the coconut filling (*inti*).*

Fold both ends of the leaf as you would when wrapping a gift.

Tuck both ends underneath the cake and arrange on a plate.

Sticky Celebration Candy (Wajik)

This is a sweet, sticky sweetmeat reserved for special occasions such as weddings and circumcision ceremonies. It is actually more like a candy than cake—very much for those with a sweet tooth!

200 g (1 cup) glutinous rice
3 tablespoons + 1 teaspoon water
150 g (1 cup) palm sugar, roughly chopped
100 ml (1/2 cup less 5 teaspoons) water
1 pandan leaf, tied into a knot
200 ml (3/4 cup + 1 tablespoon) thick coconut milk
Pinch of salt

1 Pick rice over for grit and foreign particles and wash in several changes of water until water runs clear. Soak rice overnight.

2 The following day, drain and place rice in a shallow heatproof dish or cake tin with 3 tablespoons plus 1 teaspoon water. Steam for 10 minutes before fluffing rice up with a fork. Return rice to steamer and cook for a further 20 minutes.

3 Meanwhile, heat the palm sugar and water together in a roomy pan until sugar dissolves and at least half the liquid has evaporated (this will take about 15 minutes over medium heat). Add the pandan leaf, coconut milk and salt and continue boiling for another 10 minutes.

4 Remove the pan from the heat and add the cooked rice, stirring well. Return the mixture to the stove and cook over medium heat until it reaches a thick, sticky consistency, about 10 to 15 minutes.

5 Remove the pandan leaf and turn *wajik* out into a shallow container and set aside to cool. It should be about 2 cm (1 in) thick.

6 Serve small spoonfuls of *wajik* to guests. If the *wajik* is cooked for a while longer (until the sugar starts to crystalise) it is possible to cut the cooled sweetmeat into small squares or diamond shapes, although this will produce a very sweet and hard, rather than a sticky, candy.

Makes one 17-cm (7-in) round candy
Preparation time: **15 mins + overnight soaking**
Cooking time: **60 mins**

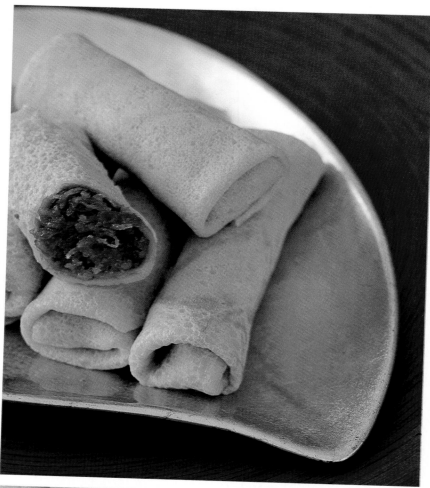

Spoon the coconut filling into the centre of each pancake.

Fold the edges in the roll up each pancake to form parcels.

Coconut Pancakes (Kuih Dadar)

150 g (1 1/4 cups) plain
flour
1/4 teaspoon salt
2 small eggs, beaten
150 ml (2/3 cup) thin
coconut milk (substitute
with plain milk)
100 ml (1/2 cup less
5 teaspoons) pandan
juice
65 ml (1/4 cup) water
1 tablespoon light
vegetable oil (such as
sunflower or soya)
1 1/2 portions coconut
filling (inti, see page 4)
2 pandan leaves for
making pandan brush
(see page 5)
Oil for greasing pan

Makes 25 pancakes
Preparation time: **1 hour**
Cooking time: **15 mins**

1 Sift flour and salt into a medium-sized mixing bowl. Make a well in the centre and into this, pour in the eggs, coconut milk and pandan juice. Using a wooden spoon or balloon whisk, gradually incorporate the flour into the liquid, making a smooth batter free from lumps. (If you somehow manage to end up with lumps in your batter, strain the mixture through a sieve.)

2 Thin the batter down with the additional 65 ml of water and stir in the oil. Mix well. Cover bowl and allow batter to stand for 20 to 30 minutes.

3 Make coconut filling (inti) according to the directions on page 4 and set aside to cool.

4 To fry pancakes, heat a small frying pan (preferably one with a non-stick surface) over medium heat. Dip pandan brush in a little oil and lightly brush your pan with it. Ensure that the pan is sufficiently hot (a drop of water should sizzle instantly).

5 Stir batter. Pour a tablespoonful of it into the pan and immediately rotate the pan so that the batter covers the base in a thin layer. Allow batter to set and just begin to brown. Flip pancake over and allow the other side to cook, just for a few seconds.

6 Turn the pancake out onto a plate or tray. Continue making the pancakes, stacking the finished ones on top of each other as you go along. As the batter tends to thicken as you cook the pancakes, you might need to thin it down with a tablespoon or two of water as you go.

7 Place a spoonful of filling in the centre of the pancake, fold both sides towards the middle and roll the pancake away from you, neatly enclosing the filling and creating a little parcel.

When making the pancakes, try to use the same scoop to ladle the batter onto the pan. Equal measures will give one more or less uniform pancakes. However, when the same scoop of batter does not spread to make the same size pancake, you know it has thickened and water needs to be added.

Durian Cake

- 150 g (5 oz) butter
- 150 g (2/3 cup) caster sugar
- 3 medium eggs, beaten
- 150 g (5 oz) fresh durian flesh, seeds removed
- 1 tablespoon milk
- 150 g (1 1/4 cup) self-raising flour, sifted

1 Line the base of an 18-cm (7-in) round or square cake tin with greaseproof paper and brush the sides lightly with softened butter. Alternatively, brush the base and sides of a fluted tube pan with softened butter. Preheat oven to 170°C (340°F).

2 Cream the butter and sugar together until light and fluffy (beating with an electric mixer, or by hand with a wooden spoon). Pour the egg in a little at a time, beating well in between additions.

3 Beat in the durian. Now switching to a large metal spoon or rubber spatula, fold in half the sifted flour, being careful not to over-stir or beat the mixture. Fold in the milk and then the remaining flour.

4 Turn the batter out into the prepared tin, hollowing it out slightly in the middle to prevent it rising to a dome in the centre. Bake cake in the preheated oven for 40 to 45 minutes or until well risen and golden brown in colour. To test if the cake is done, insert a skewer in the centre of the cake—it should come out clean, without sticky batter adhering to it.

5 When cooked, remove cake from the oven, allow it to sit in the tin for 10 minutes before turning out to cool on a wire tray.

Makes one 18-cm (7-in) cake
Preparation time: **40 mins**
Baking time: **45 mins**

Cream the butter/sugar mixture until light and fluffy.

After adding eggs and durian to the mixture, fold in the sifted flour.

Banana Cake

150 g (5 oz) very ripe
  bananas, peeled
2 teaspoon lime juice
150 g (5 oz) butter
150 g (2/3 cup) caster
  sugar
3 medium eggs, beaten
150 g (1 1/4 cup)
  self-raising flour
Pinch of bicarbonate
  of soda

1 Line the base of an 18-cm (7-in) round or square cake tin with greaseproof paper and brush the sides lightly with softened butter. Preheat oven to 170°C (340°F).

2 In a small bowl, mash the bananas with a fork and stir in the lime juice. Set aside.

3 Cream the butter and sugar together until light and fluffy (beating with an electric mixer, or by hand with a wooden spoon). Pour the eggs in a little at a time, beating well in between additions.

4 Using a large metal spoon, fold in half the flour and bicarbonate of soda without over-stirring or beating the mixture (which would otherwise toughen the cake). Fold in the mashed bananas until well incorporated and then finally, the rest of the flour.

5 Turn the mixture out into the prepared tin, hollowing out the middle slightly to prevent it rising to a dome in the middle. Bake in the preheated oven for about 40 minutes or until cake is well risen and golden brown. To test if the cake is cooked, insert a skewer in the centre—it should come out clean, without sticky batter adhering to it.

6 Allow cake to cool in the tin for 10 minutes before running a knife around the edges and turning it out to cool on a wire tray.

Makes one 18-cm (7-in) cake
Preparation time: **40 mins**
Baking time: **40–45 mins**

Steamed Layered Cake (Kuih Lapis)

160 g (1 1/2 cups) rice
flour

3 tablespoons tapioca
flour

160 g (1/2 cup + 8
teaspoons) fine
granulated white
sugar

300 ml (1 1/4 cups) thick
coconut milk

600 ml (2 1/2 cups)
water

Red colouring

Makes one 18-cm (7-in)
cake
Preparation time: **20 mins**
Cooking time: **40 mins**

1 In a mixing bowl, combine the two flours and sugar
together. Add the coconut milk and water and stir
well to make a thin batter free from lumps. Strain
batter through a fine sieve and divide the mixture
into two equal parts.

2 Keep one part white and tint the other a light pink
by adding just a drop or two of red colouring.

3 Heat a shallow 18-cm (7-in) round or square cake
tin (or heatproof dish), with straight sides, in the
steamer. Ensure steamer and tin are absolutely level.

4 Pour a thin layer of pink batter to cover the base of
the tin completely. Steam until set, about 8 minutes.
(If you pour the batter out from a measuring jug,
it is easy to note the amount of batter required, thus
ensuring that each layer you add on is of the same
thickness.)

5 Pour on the next layer of (white) batter and steam
until set. Continue adding on the layers in alternate
colours, remembering to stir the batter every time
before pouring out as rice flour has a tendency to
settle. Always use separate spoons for stirring the
different coloured batters to prevent the colours
from running into each other.

6 When you have enough batter for just one more
layer, add a few extra drops of red colouring to this
and pour it over the steamed layers, creating a bright
red top. Steam as usual.

7 When cooked, allow cake to cool completely by
sitting it in a larger container of cold water and
changing the water every time it becomes warm.
Once thoroughly cool, cut cake into 3-cm (1 1/4-in)
squares or diamond shapes.

*When using an 18-cm (7-in) round tray, a standard
1/3 cup of batter per layer gives you exactly 9 layers
resulting in a cake that is about 5 cm (2 in) high.*

Egg-shaped Cakes (Kuih Cara)

150 g (1 1/4 cups) plain
flour
1/4 teaspoon salt
2 small eggs, beaten
200 ml (3/4 cup +
1 tablespoon) thin
coconut milk (or plain
milk)
100 ml (1/2 cup less 5
teaspoons) pandan
juice (see page 4)
1 tablespoon light
vegetable oil (such as
sunflower or soya)
Oil for greasing pan
2 pandan leaves for
making pandan brush
(see page 5)
White sugar
Kuih cara mould (see
note below)

Serves 6 to 8
Preparation time: **20 mins**
Baking time: **30–40 mins**

1 Sift flour and salt into a medium-sized mixing bowl.
Make a well in the centre and pour the eggs, coconut
(or plain) milk and pandan juice. Using a wooden
spoon or balloon whisk, gradually incorporate the
flour into the liquid, making a smooth lump-free
batter. (If you can see lumps in the batter, strain the
mixture through a sieve.)

2 Heat a *kuih cara* mould over medium heat and
lightly brush with a little oil using your pandan brush.
Alternatively, heat oiled pattty tin in oven at 175°C
(340°F) until very hot. To have the required heat to
cook the base of the cake as soon as the batter hits
the pan, you can probably make 4 to 5 at a time.

3 Stir batter and half-fill the little moulds, pouring
the batter out from a jug. Carefully place half a
teaspoon of sugar in the middle of each cake, being
careful not to let it touch the sides of the mould
where it would otherwise caramelize and burn. Top
up with the rest of the batter. Put a lid on the mould
and cook until the cakes are set (about 8 to 10 minutes
on the stove top, 5 to 8 minutes in the oven).

4 Carefully remove the cakes from the mould and cool
on a wire tray. Reheat and grease the moulds or patty
tins and continue making the cakes until all the batter
is used up. Traditionally these cakes are served in
pairs, to look like eggs or flowers.

A kuih cara *mould is a heavy dish made either of brass
or aluminium that holds a series of flower or egg-
shaped depressions into which batter is poured.
Alternatively, these cakes can be baked in the oven
using small patty tins measuring 3 cm (1 1/4 in)
across the base.*

Sweetcorn Pudding

600 ml (2 1/2 cups) thin coconut milk
60 g (1/2 cup) green pea flour
180 g (3/4 cup) white sugar
1 pandan leaf, tied into a knot
300 g (10 oz) tin of cream corn

1 Combine coconut milk, flour and sugar in a pan.
Stir until well mixed. Add pandan leaf and sweetcorn.
2 Cook over low heat, stirring continuously with a
wooden spoon, until mixture boils and is thick and
smooth. Allow mixture to simmer for 3 to 4 minutes.
Take pan off the heat, remove pandan leaf.
3 Spoon mixture into small jelly moulds which have
been rinsed with water. Leave puddings to cool at
room temperature before chilling in the refrigerator.
4 Sweetcorn pudding can be served turned out of its
mould and surrounded by a spoonful of evaporated
milk.

*Alternatively, you can also pour the cooked pudding
mix into a 16-cm (6 1/2-in) glass dish or cake tin. After
a thorough chilling, cut into 3 x 3 cm squares and
serve. Pudding served this way needs to be firmer to
ensure easy cutting, So for the above recipe, increase
the quantity of green pea flour from 60 g to 75 g.*

Makes one 20-cm (8-in) ring mould
Preparation time: **10 mins**
Cooking time: **10 mins**

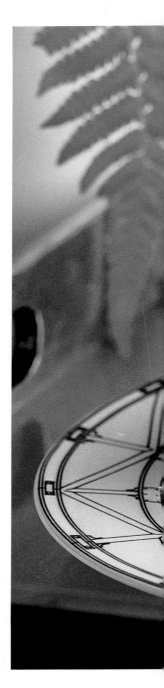

Mango Pudding

150 ml (2/3 cup) water
  (at room temperature)
3 teaspoons powdered
  gelatine
4–6 tablespoons fine
  granulated sugar
  (depending on the
  sweetness of the
  mangoes)
1 or 2 ripe mangoes,
  about 450 g (14 oz)
150 ml (2/3 cup) fresh
  or UHT milk
150 ml (2/3 cup)
  evaporated milk

1 Measure water into a heatproof bowl and sprinkle the gelatine over the water. Set aside for 10 to 15 minutes until gelatine absorbs the water and looks swollen and spongy. Melt the gelatine by sitting the bowl in a larger bowl of hot water—stir until gelatine is totally dissolved and there are no more lumps. Stir the sugar into the gelatine (if your mangoes are well-flavoured and sweet, you will need only the minimum amount of sugar, if mangoes are a little sour, you may need a little more).

2 Peel mangoes and cut the two halves away from the stone. Cut half the mango flesh into small, neat dice to obtain 150 g (5 oz) diced mango. Weigh out 170 g (5 1/2 oz) of flesh from the remaining mango and cut into rough cubes. Purée in an electric blender or food processor with the fresh milk.

3 Combine the gelatine mixture, evaporated milk, puréed mango and diced mango. Stir well and pour into small glass bowls. Chill well until set before serving.

Makes six 1/2-cup jelly moulds
Preparation time: 10 mins
Chilling time: 1 hour

Sago and Honeydew Melon in Coconut Milk

1 litre (4 cups) water
3 tablespoons pearl sago
500 ml (2 cups) thin
  coconut milk
100 g (1/3 cup + 5 tea-
  spoons) white sugar
1 pandan leaf, tied into
  a knot
400 g (13 oz) ripe
  honeydew melon
Ice cubes

Serves 5 to 6
Preparation time: 30 mins
Assembling time: 20 mins

1 Bring 1 litre (4 cups) of water to the boil in a large pan. Add the sago to the water and stir to keep the grains moving and prevent them from settling to the bottom of the pan. Cook sago for 5 minutes. Turn off heat, cover pan and set aside for 10 minutes. By then, the sago should no longer have any opaque bits, indicating that it is cooked.

2 Pour the sago into a strainer and rinse under running water to wash off excess starch, until sago grains are loose and separate. Leave sago in the sieve to drain thoroughly.

3 Place coconut milk, sugar and pandan into a pan and heat gently to boiling point. Take pan off the heat and sit it in a sink of cold water to cool. When coconut milk reaches room temperature, pour into a jug and refrigerate until ready to serve.

4 Remove skin from honeydew melon and, on a clean cutting board reserved for preparing fruit, cut flesh neatly into 1/2-cm (1/4-in) dice.

5 To serve, place a spoonful of sago and diced honeydew melon in a bowl and pour over some sweetened coconut milk. Add ice cubes and serve immediately.

Sago Pudding with Palm Sugar

3 litres (12 cups) water
200 g (1 cup) pearl sago
200 g (1 1/3 cups) palm sugar, roughly chopped
150 ml (2/3 cup) water
250 ml (1 cup) coconut milk

Makes 4 small jellies
Preparation time: **30 mins**
Chilling time: **30 mins**

1 Bring the water to the boil in a big pan. Sprinkle sago into the water and stir to keep the grains moving and prevent them from settling to the bottom of the pan. Cook sago for 10 minutes. Turn off heat, cover pan and set aside for 10 minutes. By then, the sago should no longer have any opaque bits, indicating that it is cooked.
2 Pour the sago into a strainer and rinse under running water to wash off excess starch, until sago grains are loose and separate. Leave sago in the sieve to drain thoroughly.
3 Spoon sago into rinsed jelly moulds or small dessert glasses and chill well.
4 Combine palm sugar and water in a small pan and simmer until sugar dissolves. Cool.
5 To serve, turn sago out and spoon on some coconut milk and palm sugar syrup.

Palm Sugar and Coconut Milk Jelly

500 ml (2 cups) water
180 g (1 1/4 cups) palm sugar, roughly chopped
3 teaspoons agar powder
1 pandan leaf, tied into a knot
300 ml (1 1/4 cups) thick coconut milk
Pinch of salt

Makes one round 16-cm
 (6 1/2-in) jelly
Preparation time: **15 mins**
Cooking time: **20 mins**
Chilling time: **1 hour**

1 Place water, sugar, agar powder and pandan leaf in a roomy pan and bring to the boil. Lower heat and simmer until agar powder completely dissolves, about 15 to 20 minutes.
2 Remove pandan leaf. Stir salt into the coconut milk and pour this into the jelly. Return mixture to the boil then immediately remove from heat.
3 Pour jelly into a glass dish or cake tin measuring approximately 16 cm (6 1/2 in) across and leave undisturbed until set. When cool, chill in the refrigerator. The jelly should separate nicely into 2 layers—a clear palm sugar layer on the bottom and a coconut layer on top. Cut as desired.

To hasten cooling, sit the jelly container within a larger container (such as a cake tin or in the kitchen sink) and fill with enough cold water to reach three-quarters of the way up the side of the jelly container.

Pandan Jelly

500 ml (2 cups) water
3 teaspoons agar powder
150 g (1/2 cup + 2 tablespoons) white sugar
100 ml (1/2 cup less 5 teaspoons) pandan juice
  (see page 4)
120 ml (1/2 cup) thick coconut milk
1 egg, beaten (optional)

Makes one round 16-cm
  (6 1/2-in) jelly
Preparation time: **15 mins**
Cooking time: **20 mins**
Chilling time: **1 hour**

1 Combine water, agar powder and sugar in a roomy pan and heat to boiling. Reduce heat and simmer until agar granules completely dissolve, about 15 to 20 minutes.

2 In a bowl, combine the pandan juice, coconut milk and egg (if using, the egg gives a richer jelly but does not affect the taste), beating with a fork to ensure they are well mixed.

3 Pour this into the simmering jelly, stirring constantly and then wait for the mixture to come back to the boil. Once it reaches a rolling boil, take the pan off the heat immediately and pour contents into a shallow glass dish or cake tin measuring approximately 16 cm (6 1/2 in) across. Set aside to cool thoroughly before chilling in the refrigerator. Cut as desired.

Bread Pudding

1 tablespoon softened butter
2 eggs
80 g (1/3 cup + 1 teaspoon) white sugar
200 ml (3/4 cup) coconut milk
150 ml (2/3 cup) plain milk
A few drops vanilla extract
6 slices white bread, cut into 3-cm (1 1/4-in) squares
50 g (1/3 cup) golden sultanas
Extra sugar for sprinkling

Makes one 15-cm (6-in) round
  pudding
Preparation time: **15 mins**
Soaking time: **30 mins**
Cooking time: **40 mins**

1 Lightly brush the base and sides of a shallow 15-cm (6-in) heatproof dish with softened butter; set aside. Preheat oven to 180°C (350°F).
2 In a medium-sized bowl, beat the eggs and sugar together and pour in the coconut and plain milk. Flavour with a few drops of vanilla extract. Add the bread and sultanas to this mixture and set aside for 20 to 30 minutes, stirring the bread occasionally to ensure even soaking.
3 Turn mixture out into the buttered container and spread out evenly. Sprinkle on a tablespoon of sugar on the top and bake for 30 to 40 minutes or until golden brown. Cool before cutting into 3-cm (1 1/4-in) squares for serving.

Index